I0196352

The Birthday Party to Which Nobody Came

ISBN 1-928561-14-4

Copyright © 2019 by Stewart Marshall Gulley

All rights reserved. No part of this publication may be reproduced, distributed, or transmitted in any form or by any means, including photocopying, recording, or other electronic or mechanical methods, without the prior written permission of the publisher, except in the case of brief quotations embodied in critical reviews and certain other noncommercial uses permitted by copyright law.

For permission requests, write to the publisher, addressed Attention: Permissions Coordinator," at the address below Stewart Marshall Gulley P.O. Box 2063 Los Angeles, California 90078 www.stewartmarshallgulley.com

I dedicate this book to my sister Gwendolyn Marshall

This book belongs to

_____

_____

_____

o———————————————o

Date

o———————————————o

From

The Birthday Party To Which Nobody Came!

(Based on a true story)
by Stewart Marshall Gulley

It had been a beautiful month in Newark, New Jersey, and it was going to be Butch's 11th birthday on November 25th. He was quite a happy kid and was showed love all year long. He never recalled having a birthday party when he was younger, so this would be something special. There was nothing there for him to look forward to or make a big fuss about when it came to parties. Usually, his birthday was around Thanksgiving, and the holiday preparation would always interfere, but it never really bothered him because he knew he would get something special.

This year was going to be a different year, he thought to himself, as he told his mother that he wanted to have a party. She agreed and knew there had to be some preparations to be made--things like food, decorations, invitations and everything else that went with a party.

Happy Birthday

Butch had some older sisters and brothers that had moved out. Though he was from a family of nine children, only the three younger ones remained in the house at that time. They were Butch, Gwen, and Wynakee. While the preparations were taking place, invitations were made and were given out as well as a few phone calls were made.

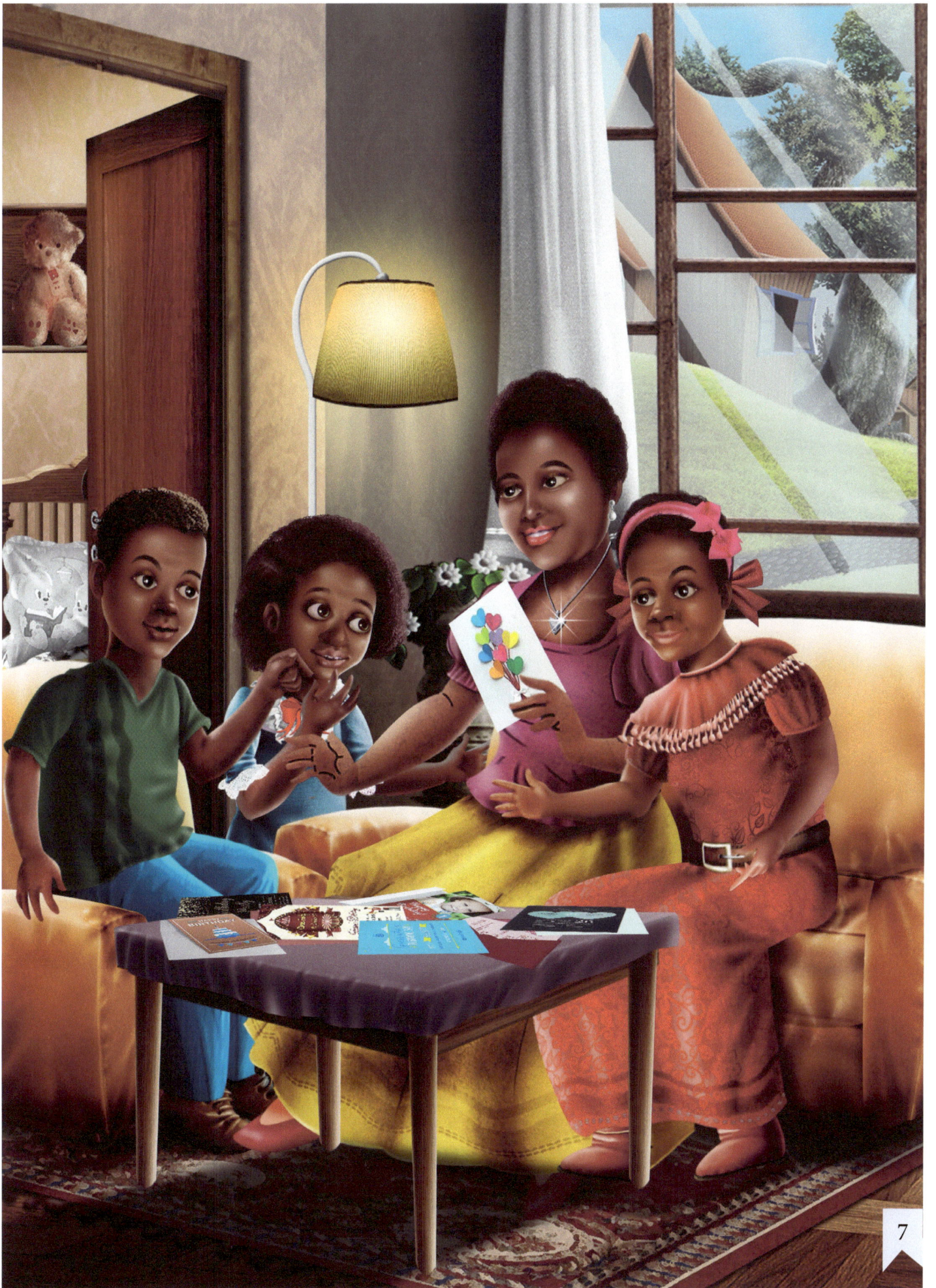

Just the day before,
he remembered his mother
telling him that the
weatherman had said that
there might be rain the
following day, but it
may not be that bad
for an indoor party.

Mother ordered the cake, bought hotdogs, hamburgers and supplied all of the condiments needed for an enjoyable party. Butch, Gwen and Wynakee put up the balloons and the other decorations for the party.

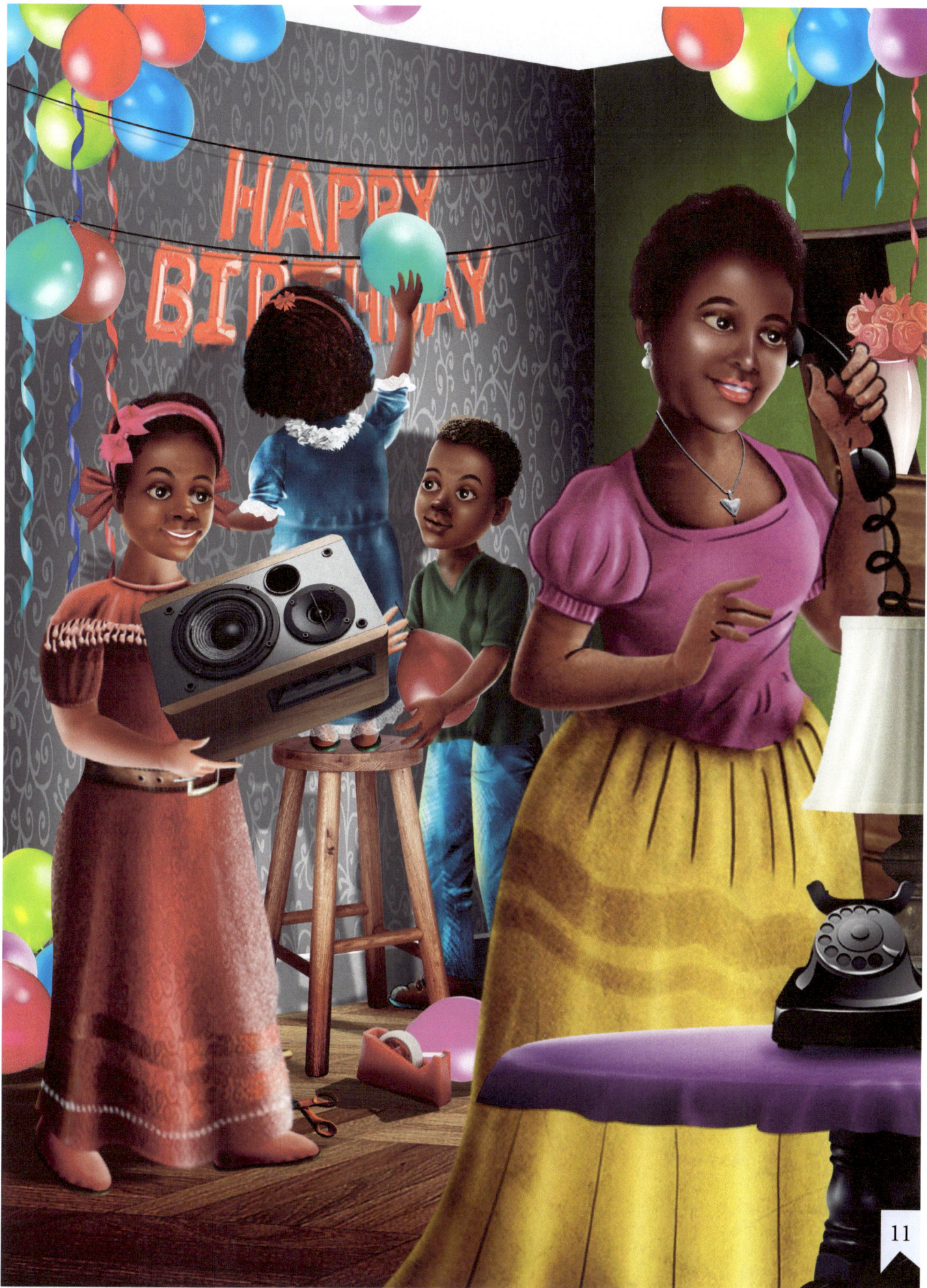

Everything was fine that morning, and then suddenly, there came some drizzles. Butch looked out the window, hoping it would stop because he was expecting a friendly little crowd. But it began to rain, and then it rained harder and he and his sisters were wondering when the rain was going to stop. The party was supposed to start at 2 pm, but there was no one there but Butch and his two sisters and their mother.

"Maybe the rain will taper down son," his mother said as she was trying to give him hope. Unfortunately, it rained even more. It rained so hard you could barely look out of the window.

Now it was about 5 o'clock, and it was still raining. Butch had to accept that there wasn't going to be a party. His mother felt sorry for him and wanted to comfort him. Still, somehow she knew he was a mentally strong kid and didn't need many people to help him have fun. He was a loner and had fun creating things with his hands. But this particular day, he was expecting company.

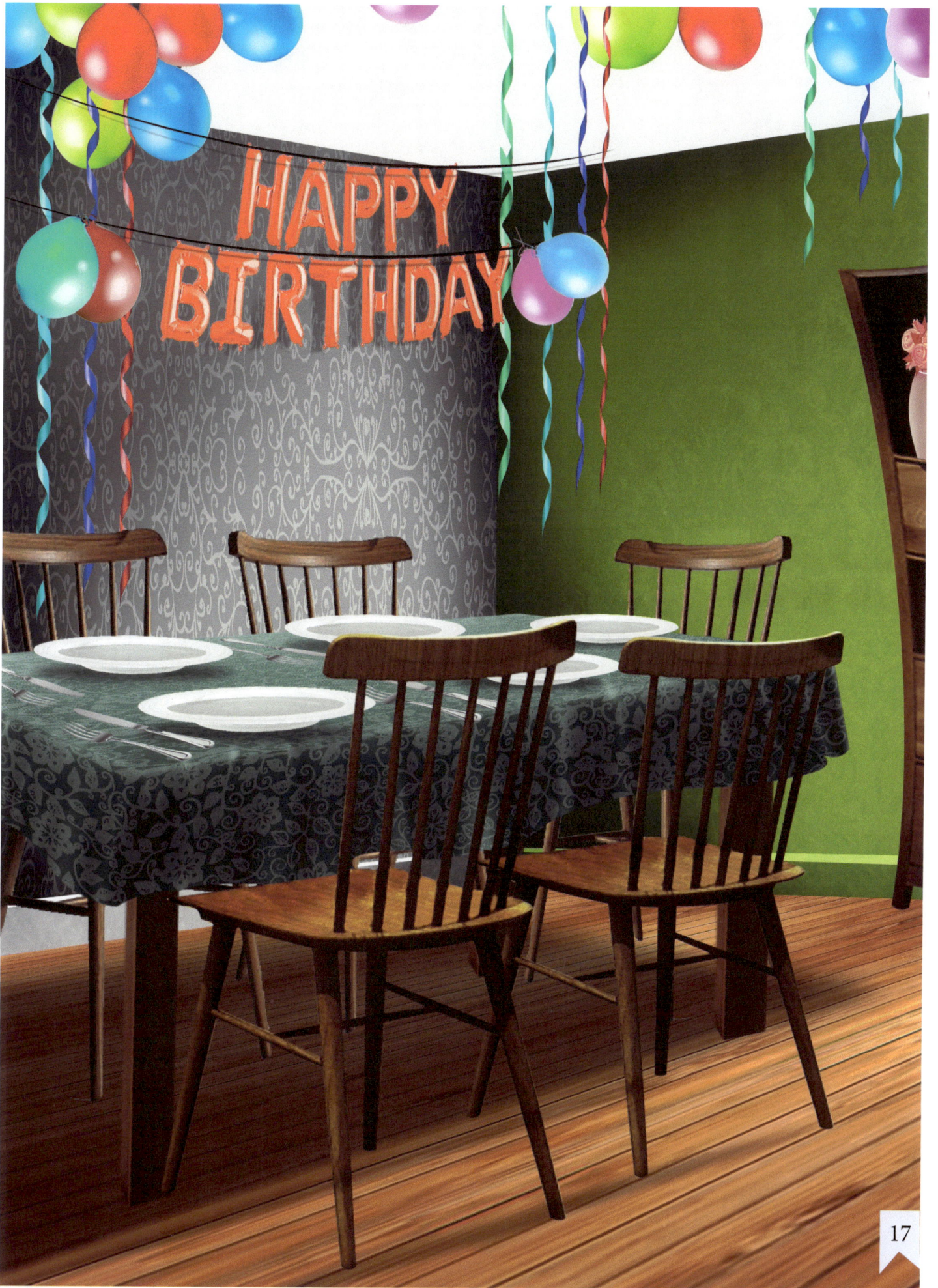

There were no children; there were no games played, there were no gifts, not even one phone call saying their child wasn't coming because of the rain. It was just Butch and his sisters. Butch looked out the window with a little sadness in his eyes.

But after thinking a while, he said "I will just have a party with my sisters, and we will eat all of the food and cake we want. We can eat until we burst," and the three of them just laughed and played. Butch loved birthday cakes, and he ate as much as he wanted, and his sisters ate as much as they wanted to. They all had a great time. Later, he figured, having a party must put a lot of pressure on people because they have to prepare for it and others have to go through the trouble of trying to bring something to the birthday celebrant.

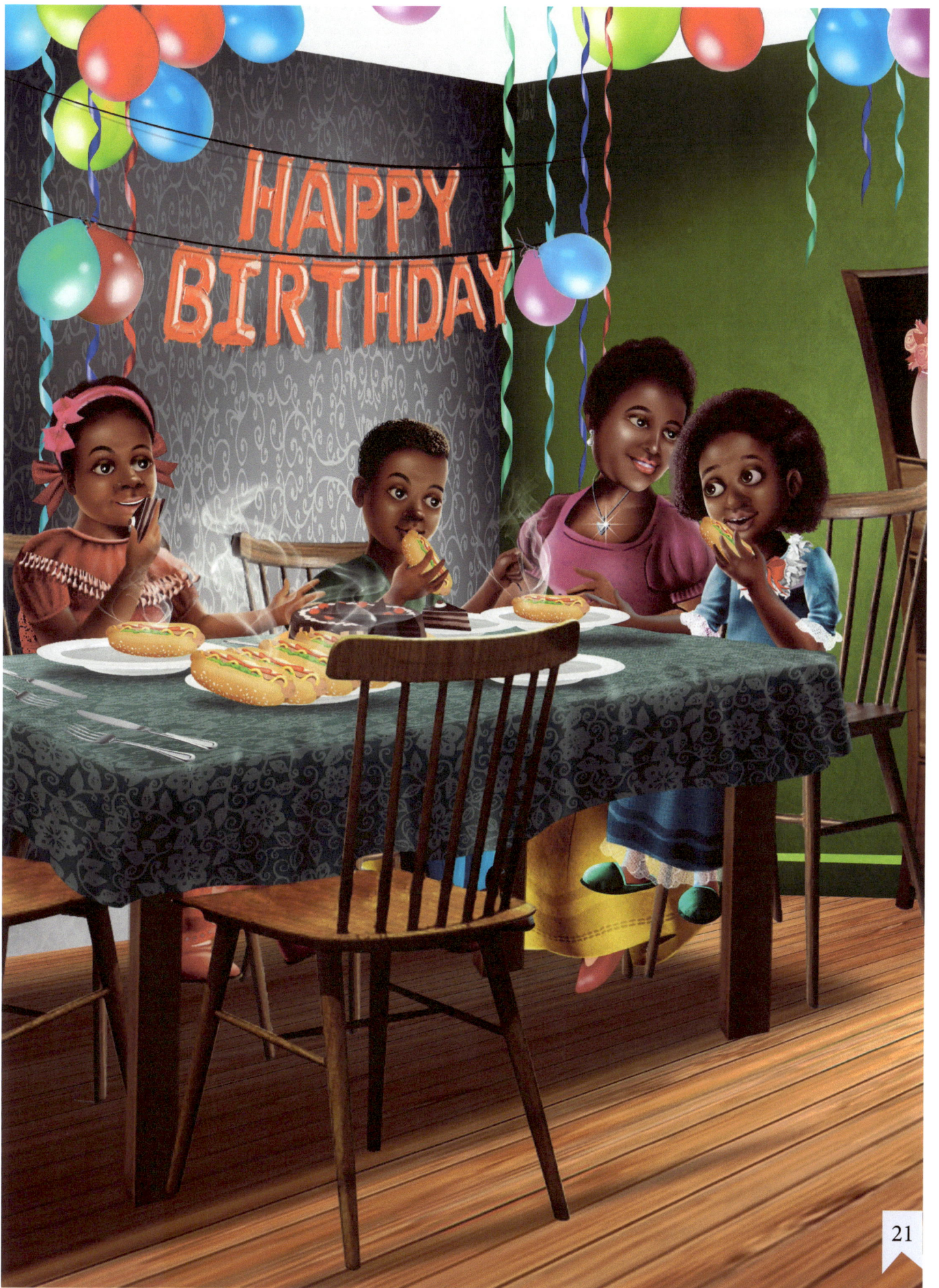

Maybe that's why they didn't come, because of the work involved. Who would take the extra time out for me, he thought? He even thought about Christmas, and he felt that it was almost the same, as people would expect to receive something because they gave a gift, and they may not receive one in return, which could bring about a big disappointment. What was supposed to be a joyful holiday then becomes a depressing day. It can even be disappointing that someone didn't spend as much money on their gift for you as you did for theirs. Well, 58 years went by, and Butch refused to have a birthday party because he felt that no one would come. Also, he didn't want to pressure anyone to celebrate his day with him or force or burden them to bring a gift for him.

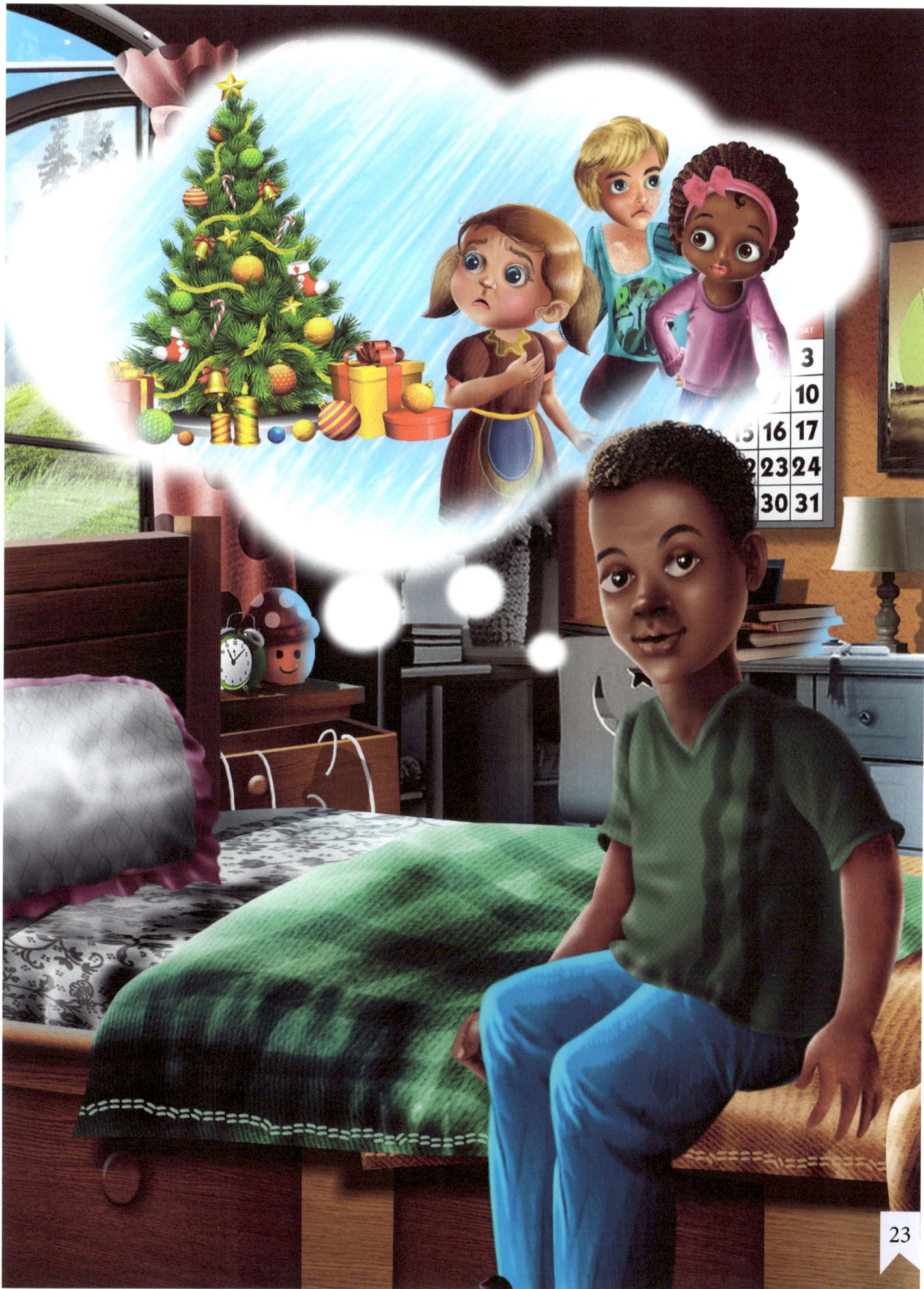

Butch decided that he didn't have to wait 365 days to have a party or wait to be invited to someone else's party for some birthday cake. He would help himself to some cake whenever he felt like it. Sometimes when Butch wanted a cake, he'd sit in his favorite chair and call the bakery to place an order so he could pick it up. Even though Butch knew how to make all sorts of cake, there was something special about him ordering a birthday cake that made him happy.

Every now and then, he would buy a slice of cake at the market or buy a whole one and put his name on it anytime that he would like. If he needed something special, he would save some money and get it as a gift for himself. Why wait for a particular day, when every day can already be special when you're having fun? I can have cake anytime I wanted, all year long, and if I needed a gift, I could treat myself to one any day of any year. Just because it's March, I don't have to wait until my birthday in November to get something.Who says that my friends or I will be around in November? So, why should I wait to celebrate my birthday once a year?

Every day I wake up, I consider my birthday, and I celebrate that I'm alive. And to this day, anyone who knows him knows that he loves birthday cakes and he will eat them all year round---party or no party! Butch's message to everyone: "Never depend on anyone else for your happiness, because your happiness cannot start from anywhere else other than from deep within yourself. Everyone does not respect RSVP on your invitation."

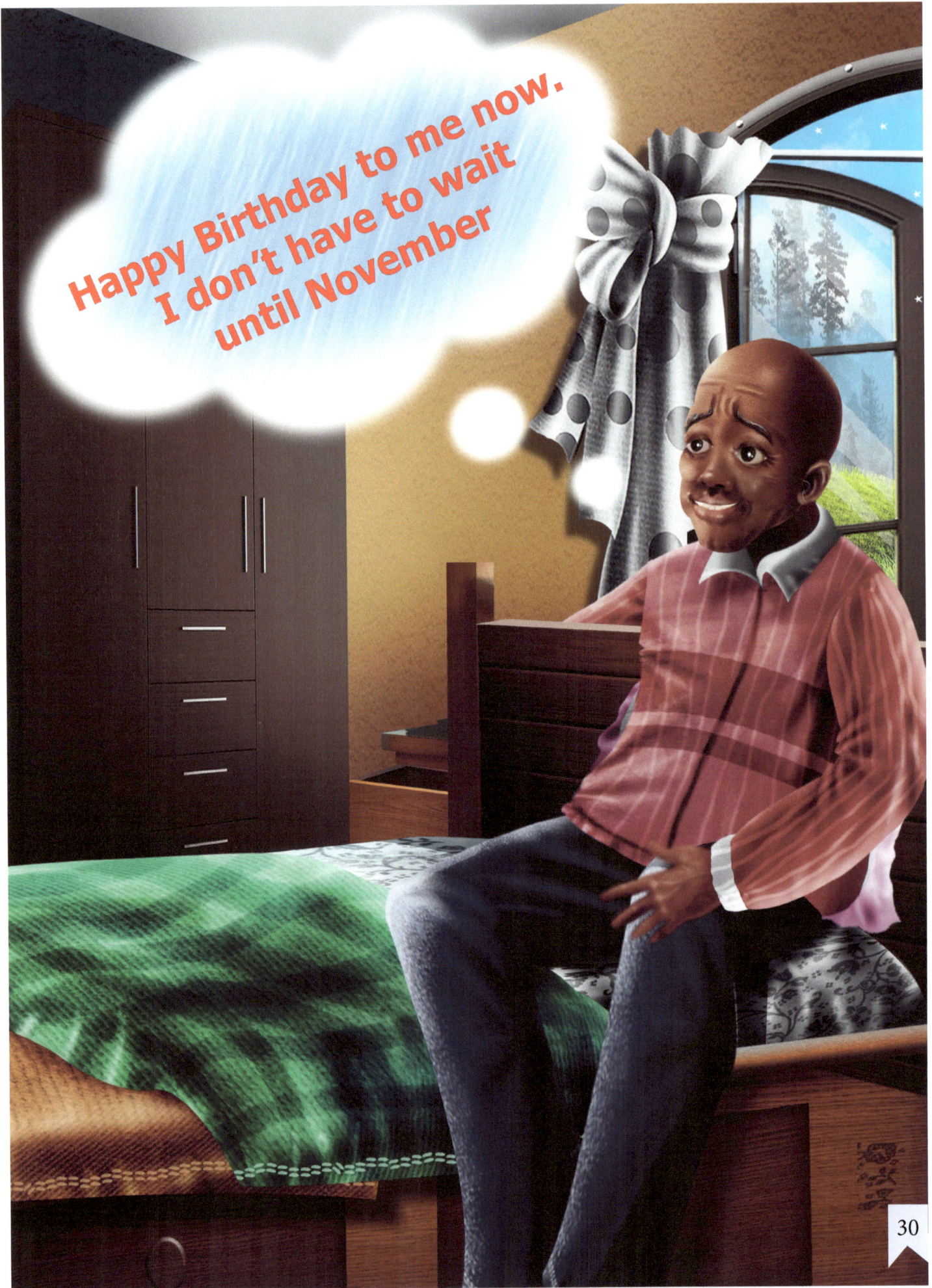

A Birthday Prayer

I am having a birthday party
And I hope to see you there
There will be fun and dancing
And smiles just everywhere

I hope you won't be busy
To share this day with me
I am preparing it just for YOU
Some things you won't believe

I've put a lot of thought into this
As I wrote your name
To me, you are so unique
And you'll be glad you came

If for some unseen reason
That you cannot come
I will have to shift my joy a little
Because I will miss your pleasant fun

Know that I will miss your smile
Your happy birthdays too
With everything that I prepared
I always thought of you

But do me this big favor
And don't you feel ashamed
Call me, or drop a letter
So I'll be prepared to miss your name

That would mean so much to me
And I will still keep my glow
I'd hate to feel the pain of no warning
That if you did not show

I'd keep looking out the window
Looking for the ones I know
But your courtesy will astound me
Because at least you let me know

You freed yourself of feeling guilty
Which was not my intention at all
But peace will happen for both of us
By making just that one call

P.S. The best gift you could ever bring is yourself, and it's priceless!

YOUR FRIEND FOREVER!

- Stewart Marshall Gulley

What is RSVP?

The term "RSVP" comes from the French expression répondez s'il vous plaît, meaning "please respond." If RSVP is written on an invitation, it means the host has requested that the guest respond to say if they plan to attend the party. It shows respect to the host of whether or not to prepare for you. After all, they thought enough to invite you, and having a party that no one comes can be devastating

Please RSVP

By_____

Date

_____

Name

____**Happily accepts**   ____**Sad to miss it**

Posted on Butch's front door after all of these years!

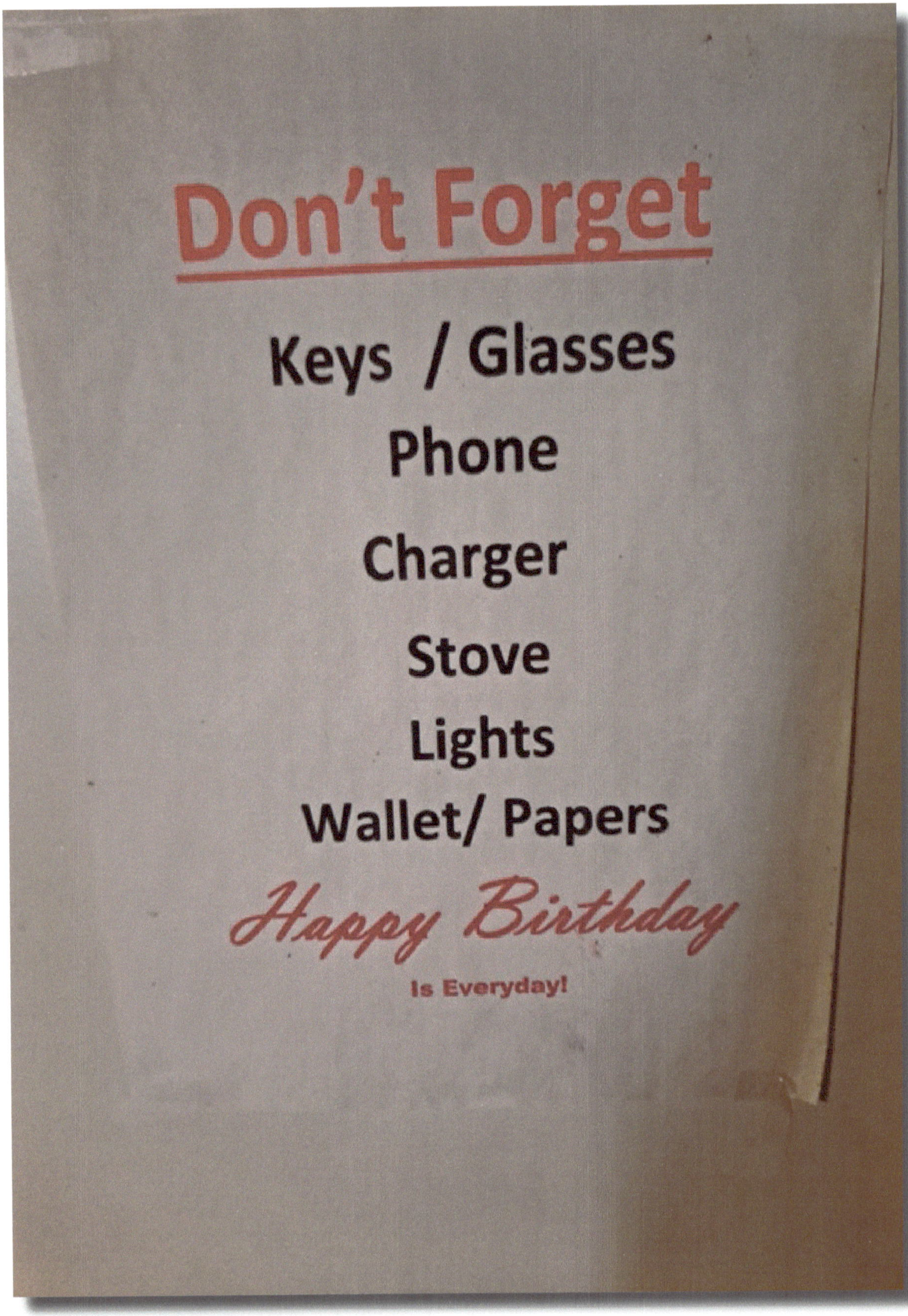

Don't Forget

Keys / Glasses

Phone

Charger

Stove

Lights

Wallet/ Papers

Happy Birthday

Is Everyday!

Other children books by Stewart Marshall Gulley

His Eye Is On the Sparrow
*(Children's Coloring & Storybook with Comprehension Test-
Looking out for one another)*

The Elephant and the Mouse
(An unlikely story about a true friendship)

The Witch that Got a Miracle
(The importance of fruits & vegetables)

The Dog, The Man and The Cat
(Keeping your friends looking good)

The Lizard and the Frog
(Teaching one another)

***

Also Self-Help and novels for adults

Available Amazon.com

More coming! The Alphabet and Counting!

BIOGRAPHY- STEWART MARSHALL GULLEY,

best selling author, has been often called The Renaissance Man because of his many professional talents. A producer, playwright, author, real estate agent, cosmetology instructor, auctioneer and inspirational speaker are only a partial list of his phenomenal gifts and accomplishments. He gave it all up to write books for children and adults. Many see him as a very comical person and most agree he should have been a stand-up comedian; however, his serious side manages to come through his self-help, non-fiction and fiction books. An exceptionally versatile writer."The Birthday Party to Which Nobody Came," was a true story based on one of the events in the earlier years of his personal life, which he will never forget. He has learned to make himself happy as much as he possibly can, and strangely enough, all those around him become happy as well because of his sense of humor and positive views on life.

"When your party starts with you, even when others don't show up, you're guaranteed to still have a good party."
- Stewart Marshall Gulley

Butch at 11 years old.

36

FAMILY BIRTHDAYS

Name   Relationship   Birthday

SPECIAL OCCASION DAYS

Name of the event   `   When   Where

www.ingramcontent.com/pod-product-compliance
Lightning Source LLC
Chambersburg PA
CBHW042125040426

42450CB00002B/72

9 781928 561149